GW01417748

Ekard Li

TEAM–dance

A Guide to Canine Freestyle

Photography: Marie-Therese,
Maria and Ekard Lind

BARRON'S

CONTENTS

4

Human-Canine Relationship

CONCEPTUAL SUPERSTRUCTURE:

Ethics + Ethology
+ Pedagogy + Sport
+ Individuality
} = "Alignment"

Human-Canine Harmony

PRACTICAL STRUCTURE:

Communication
+ Motivation
+ Play + Authority
} = "LIND-ART"

TEAM-balance
training and athletic preparation

TEAM-work
trained athletes working together

TEAM-sport
Structured competition
at four levels.
Separate class
for seniors.

TEAM-dance
Structured competition
at four levels.
Separate class
for seniors.

Transforming the Human–Canine Relationship

The essential difference between TEAM-dance and conventional training methods is that TEAM-dance focuses less on obedience than on the skillful encouragement of performance. That is, the goals of the human become the goals of the dog as well. The fundamental principles of TEAM-dance are based on sound behavioral research about how animals learn. The dog is no longer "trained" as a tool of the handler; instead, its own natural needs are taken seriously. The "dog handler" thus becomes the "team leader," and the "obedient" dog is now a (canine) member of an athletic team, performing the expected tasks with joy and active involvement.

TEAM-dance represents the culmination of a dog training system developed by Ekard Lind and trademarked as LIND-art. The system incorporates up-to-date knowledge in the field of animal pedagogy and includes new practical methods, such as the effective timing of signals, motivational balance, mental aids and guidance, as well as concepts such as saturation distance, impulsive touch, and passive influence.

The term LIND-art itself reflects Lind's distinctive holistic approach, centered on a clear understanding of the ethical imperatives of the human–canine relationship, along with an affirmation that in each and every interaction with dogs, humans should respect the nature of the canine species. The ultimate goal is to take the age-old ideal of human–canine harmony and transform it into a new reality for today's world.

Upon this foundation was born a new form of canine sport, whose central concept is known as TEAM-work. Combined under this concept are the two disciplines of TEAM-sport and TEAM-dance.

TEAM-work is unlike the traditional "obedience" competition, with its emphasis on highly structured formal evaluations. Rather, TEAM-work focuses mainly on harmonious social communication as "qualitative performance"—without equipment aids and without any measurements of time, height, or distance.

TEAM-sport is further enhanced in TEAM-dance. Here, music, rhythm, tone, and form are brought to bear as additional resources in the quest for human–canine harmony.

WHY
TEAM-dance?

- Moving to music with your TEAM partner dog is fun.

- Freestyle dance takes many and varied forms.

- Dances can be choreographed individually to capitalize on a breed's strengths.

- Dance opens a new realm of communication and interaction between human and dog.

- Freestyle develops your artistry, imagination, and creativity.

- Dancing enhances the dog's natural conformation and movement.

- TEAM-dance requires no special equipment or other people to help.

- You can enjoy TEAM-dance anywhere, at any time of year.

- Dancing is a healthy way for humans and dogs of any age to exercise.

- TEAM-dance offers a broad spectrum of competition, with 4 levels, 3 classes, and 5 sections, as well as connections to TEAM-sport and other canine disciplines.

Many people enjoy listening to music. What could be more natural than to take this a step further, enhancing the experience of music by actively reproducing it in movement? And if you enjoy spending leisure time with your dog and listening to music at the same time, why not combine the two?

Dancing in partnership with your dog creates a special kind of harmony. You'll find it both fascinating and profound to experience the way music, rhythm, words, sounds, and form flow together, creating an interplay that is thoroughly satisfying for both of you. The invigorating and harmonizing powers of music will resonate with anyone who is open to them. Naturally, the atmosphere that music creates also enhances the performance itself. Music definitely contributes to the relaxed and positive mood in which handler and dog approach each other. Dancing together to music is immensely pleasurable, and it won't get boring, even after years and years. Every dance is different, and every handler can create a unique freestyle presentation and learn it with his or her own dog. Choreographing a presentation allows elements of freedom that are not present in any other form of canine performance.

A unique feature of TEAM-dance is that older dogs in particular show great talent and skill. Recognizing this, TEAM-dance—for the first time ever in canine competition—instituted a special "Senior Class." Another innovation is the establishment of four instead of three performance levels, allowing finer distinctions between the requirements; novices can perform at a much lower level, while top performances can rise to a much higher standard.

TYPICAL TEAM

Both humans and wolves are capable of living alone. Both, however, are stronger when living in community. Similarities in the societal structures of humans and wolves, together with beneficial ecological changes, set the stage for a partnership that is unique in history.

The questions of when the bond between human and dog was first formed, and whether it was the human or the wolf that took the initiative in this liaison, are beyond the scope of this discussion. It is known that the dog is the oldest animal companion of humans and that both profited from this partnership. The dog of early times gained safety, warmth, and especially food. Humans warmed themselves against the dog's coat; they used dogs in hunting, to pull sleds, and as watchdogs, but also as companions (and as an emergency source of food). The remarkable adaptability of the dog made possible a wide variety of specialized tasks, which in turn led to the development and refinement of ever more and newer breeds of dogs, from the fighting dog to shipboard companions. Even today, despite industrialization and the proliferation of technology, dogs have not lost their appeal. Quite the opposite; new tasks—from sniffing out contraband drugs to providing therapeutic support—bear witness to the unbroken significance of the human–canine partnership.

Although this relationship is very old, each generation of humans has seen it differently. A common thread, of course, has always been the concept of the "happy dog"—a term used long ago by the Greek historian Xenophon (ca. 430–354 B.C.) and recurring in every generation. The understanding of what this means in concrete terms, however, or how this ideal is translated into reality, has differed considerably from one generation to the next. Even in our time, the concept of the "happy dog" is seen in a new light, as we analyze whether and how the ideal image of the human–canine relationship can be realized.

Behavioral research, a relatively young science, has taught us that despite the wide variety of canine breeds and despite the dog's long history of domestication, the dog "in the essence of its being remains a wolf" (Eric Zimen). What we know about behavior has brought about a wide range of changes in our understanding of the human–canine relationship.

Also a factor is the discovery of emotional intelligence—the recognition that feelings can significantly influence mental performance—as well as other newly defined systems of intelligence. In our view, this has already shed a new and brighter light on the intelligent performance of higher animals. It seems only natural that this new insight will lead to changes not

TYPICAL
TEAM

only in traditional training methods, but also in the underlying views of the human–canine relationship.

One response to the challenge of developing a contemporary human–canine relationship is the TEAM concept, whose highest expression is the ideal of human–canine harmony. If the human and the dog are mutually responsive to each other, the needs of each will be met. As long as they live together according to rules that reflect the natural rights of each, and as long as the precepts of the human–canine relationship are aimed at the ideal of human–canine harmony, there is no danger that one of the two partners in this community will be exploited or come to harm.

Even if the path from the ideal to the real is a long and difficult one, evidence from the fields of cynology (the study of the dog's natural history), behavioral biology, and animal pedagogy suggests that the TEAM concept is here to stay, not only in regard to the family dog, but in all the manifestations of the human–canine relationship, including sporting

dogs and utility dogs. However, this change in awareness will also lead to definite changes in the way humans interact with dogs.

The TEAM concept suggests that in dog training, the expectation of performance should no longer be limited to formal levels. We must recognize that learning means more than simply having the dog do what we expect; we must realize that learning means life. The TEAM concept places the "how" of communication in the foreground. This means that we must feel our way into our dog's unique nature, into its individuality; we must take its needs into account better, and we must make real use of the comprehensive pedagogical theory available to us, along with its practical applications in training.

Many other considerations argue in favor of incorporating the TEAM concept into dog training. Here is just one example: When two dogs tussle over an object, at first glance it seems that they are playfully (or seriously) disputing possession of the object. Upon closer examination, however, it is generally clear that what is really at stake, either in play or in earnest, is the social structure. Underlying the tug-of-war itself are any number of social behavior patterns and situational motives. The trainer who focuses only on the task at hand misses the point that in nature, learning and life are inextricably intertwined. As a result, rich and valuable pedagogical opportunities will surely be lost.

TYPICAL DANCE

Dancing, like singing, painting, molding clay, or simply gesticulating, is one of the oldest forms of human expression. Long before children learn to talk, they are dancing freely to rhythm and music. Musical expression is part of our development as humans; we express our inner needs in music, just as the blackbird does in sending forth its song. Both humans and animals need opportunities for emotional expression; if these opportunities are lacking or suppressed, the whole organism suffers. In their wholehearted identification with rhythm and dance, children and adolescents demonstrate that such emotional forms of expression are natural, even elemental. By contrast, adults have traded in these original connections for the conventions of civilization and for a decidedly rational concept of the self. Precisely for this reason, it is important for adults to turn to music to maintain their vigor and youthfulness. We now know that music, dance, and the creative arts not only promote musical and creative achievements, but also enhance mental performance.

But even if we look only at the goal of maintaining physical health, dance will still be essential, because in dance all the muscles and joints of the body are exercised actively and in unequalled balance.

In short: There is much in favor of dancing—
for humans. But what about for dogs? Is it
really in a dog's nature to
dance? When we make
dogs dance, aren't we
forcing them to do some-
thing they would never do on
their own? Isn't dancing with dogs
just a new form of anthropomorphism? These
questions should be taken seriously, especially
by those who have dedicated themselves to
studying and valuing the nature of the dog as
a species.

To begin, it must be clearly stated that the
risks just listed do indeed exist—especially when
dancing with dogs is done carelessly, without
thought or reflection.

T Y P I C A L
DANCE

What can dancing do for dogs?

Dogs need exercise, movement, stimulation of all their senses; they need challenges and the opportunity to prove their worth. They need activity and rest, free play and interaction with other dogs. But more than that, they need closeness, security, loving attention, social contact, and acceptance into the community—and this is exactly what dancing can offer. In dance, communication and mutual attention are essential for success. Uninterrupted observation of the partner is a key element of dance, and nowhere else is friendly interaction so intensely supported.

Thus, dance emphasizes a natural element that is as typical of dogs as it is of humans—integration into the community.

Dance also has much to offer in regard to variety and adaptability. Clearly, variability and diversity are closer to the demands of life than uniform repetition (stereotypy) and automation. Unlike in traditional obedience competitions, for example, where stereotypy and automation determine the course of trials and tournaments, in canine freestyle each movement requires a new and different adaptation. Each dance thus becomes an individual and unique presentation, offering many times the diversity and richness of exercise seen in an obedience demonstration.

Little motivates a dog more than movement. Dance offers that, too. No other form of sport covers such a broad spectrum of psychomotor needs. In this connection, the argument is often put forward that slow movement, for example, is unnatural for a dog, as is backing or pivoting. These assertions are mistaken.

Wolves, wild dogs, and even domestic dogs use all three forward gaits, as well as backing and pirouetting. Furthermore, it has been found that dogs who have learned in freestyle to back, for example, will use this new way of movement on their own in daily life when it is to their advantage to do so.

Nevertheless, it would be a mistake to deny or trivialize the risk of making unnatural demands. Here it is helpful to remember the pedagogical orientation toward" integral motivation" (E. Lind). According to this principle, the "reward" of learning does not come only after a task has been mastered; rather, the act of learning itself is imbued with joy. "Practice is play!" And in TEAM-dance, dancing itself is developed from play.

In addition to this are motivations that are triggered by rhythm and sound. Even though much more research can be done about the ability of animals to experience rhythm and sound, it has already been demonstrated that dogs, like horses, have a natural talent for adjusting their stride, gait, and movement to music and rhythm. And this activity brings them pleasure.

IS TEAM-DANCE FOR YOU?

1 If you enjoy listening to music—if it moves your spirit—you already have the most important element of TEAM-dance. Everything else can be learned. The dance requirements in TEAM-dance levels 1 and 2 are anything but stringent.

2 As prerequisites, you and your dog should successfully complete a preliminary course in TEAM-balance (which lasts about 6 months). Then you and your dog are ready to start with TEAM-dance. Playful learning and the principle of small and smaller steps in learning also characterize the dance method.

3 If you already participate in a discipline with defined movements in a traditional form of obedience competition and now also want to participate in TEAM-dance, you should use different signals in the two disciplines.

4 To be successful, you should practice every day, and very briefly at first—once or twice a day, for 5 to at most 10 minutes (possibly a little longer, depending on the maturity of the dog and the amount of playing involved).

5 How long does it take to learn? Keep in mind that the dog must first spend 6 months in the preliminary stage of TEAM-balance. After that, expect to spend 8 to 12 months each for TEAM-dance levels 1 and 2; level 3 takes 1 to 1½ years. Level 4 is difficult to reach, and training for level 4 is never completed.

6 How expensive is the basic equipment? If the place where you practice has electricity, all you need is a simple tape recorder. Better is a CD player or mini-disk player (see page 44).

7 Can a person learn to do this without taking a course? Yes, it's possible. But most people need help, because these new disciplines require a considerable amount of knowledge and skill and must be developed very carefully.

8 You can also participate in trials and tournaments. See page 62 for the addresses of canine freestyle organizations, which provide support for competitors, judges, and local groups and clubs.

UNDERSTANDING THE DISCIPLINE OF TEAM-DANCE

More and more dog owners are looking for a way to interact with their dogs as partners, without rigid training methods. TEAM-dance offers a new discipline, which was born out of play and motivation and yet presents remarkable challenges.

History of TEAM-dance

In the late 1980s, individual dog trainers in Canada and Europe began to enrich traditional obedience classes and competitions with musical accompaniment. Eventually, in many countries at the same time and in many different forms, this led to the development of canine freestyle, a discipline in which the dog and handler perform to music.

In the early 1990s, the author of this book began to develop his own form of dance. Although he had recognized early on that the traditional canine disciplines were in some respects no longer in tune with the times, he chose not to publicize his development of new disciplines in its early phases or by stages as a work in progress. Only when the entire training program was complete, with TEAM-balance as the preliminary stage and the dual disciplines of TEAM-sport and TEAM-dance building on that, and a set of rules had been formulated, did he introduce his work to the public in the fall of 1998.

All breeds of dog are suitable for the new discipline of TEAM-dance.

The first public performance of the LIND-art Company took place on October 19, 1998, in Zurich, Switzerland; a second followed in Kaiserslautern, Germany, in October, and a third on November 28, 1998 in Vienna, Austria. Since then, seminars in TEAM-sport and TEAM-dance have been offered. More and more clubs and dog training schools see the programs of LIND-art as the canine education of the future and are designing their curriculum accordingly. To meet the enormous requirements of this movement, steps were taken in 1999 to found an organization for the promotion of TEAM-sport and TEAM-dance (TEAM-work-Zentrum, TWZ). In conjunction with prominent representatives of various disciplines, this organization will coordinate the training of handlers and judges as well as the holding of trials and tournaments.

Development in Harmony

TEAM-dance is based, on the one hand, on the tradition of classical obedience competition, equine dressage, and various forms of dance, and on the other hand on alternative training methods, new canine sport expectations, and on the idea of replacing stereotypical sequences with variable ones.

An important motivation for TEAM-dance was the ideal of human–canine harmony (see page 11): Not that the dog would dance, by performing one trick after another and being rewarded for it, but that the *team* would interact with each other in communication and artistic movement. The human is here not only (or primarily) as the handler, but a *dancer*. In TEAM-dance, following the model of ballroom dancing or pairs figure skating, the elements of the performance are divided equally between the two partners. The dog experiences the dance differently than the human, and thus in many respects might be subject to excessive or inappropriate demands. But the fact of the different sphere of experience does not rule out partnership in the dance; it merely places certain limits on it. In that light, the focus on human–canine harmony takes on a second important meaning: Harmony is one of the most elementary needs of the dog!

Whether with food, a toy, contact, or movement, the handler must always hold the dog's attention.

Communication for the Dance

Furthermore, the human–canine dance must be crafted in such a way that it is within the dog's experience. Interpretation and artistic expression must be transformed. But how?

The dog is capable of sensing the atmosphere created by the music and the handler and converting this mood into movement. In addition, the dog can respond to rhythm and act it out. With support and assistance from the human, the dog can develop and refine this ability.

For this reason, TEAM-dance sets particular value on a sustained positive atmosphere, in that the handler always strives to transform the positive effect of the music into communication and motion. This means more than maintaining eye contact with the dog; the positive mood is reinforced by the tone of the verbal cues. When these are used to engage the dog in movements that are appropriate to the particular breed—whether walking, trotting, galloping, leaping, or in variable sequences—the dog is motivated on many levels.

Models for TEAM-dance

Because this form of dance follows the models of ballroom dancing and pairs figure skating, and because the dog can execute only a limited spectrum of the dance itself, communication between the dance partners and their movement in concert become more important. "Movement in concert in the dance" means that the maneuvers are performed by dog and human together. Therefore, from the start TEAM-dance has emphasized the conveyance of a sustained positive mood (supported by verbal cues) as well as variosynchronicity (see pages 23, 59).

Traditional obedience competition, with its demand for athletic precision and reliability, was also an important model for TEAM-dance

from the start. This link to the traditional obe-dience repertoire is also found, by the way, in other forms of canine freestyle.

Artistic Elements

Another key element of TEAM-dance has always been music. Despite its carefully con-sidered limitations, TEAM-dance was not envisioned as merely a sport, but was intended as dance—that is, with essential aesthetic and artistic elements, and with the athletic achievements subordinated to the music and choreography.

This artistic element, however, brings further consequences:

✔ For the human dancer, the body is the

The canine partner seeks eye contact with the human handler even when the latter is not holding a motivational object.

instrument. However, if the arms and hands are occupied with holding and managing treats or other motivational objects, then a part of this instrument, and indeed a very important part, is diverted for another purpose. Meanwhile, the dog is most likely thinking only of the tasty morsel or the motivational object and is no longer communicating on the level of a mood shared with the handler. As a result, the dance suffers a shift that alienates it from its goal.

During a performance, the dog must be able to ignore any distractions.

In TEAM-dance, this is done:
✔ by uninterrupted positive motivation and emotionality during the dance;
✔ by constant communication using audible cues instead of visible signals, leaving the body free for the dance and for artistic expression;
✔ by variosynchronous pace alternating with figures and interludes of trot or gallop;
✔ by weaving games into the training process;
✔ by careful, playful teaching of the maneuvers;
✔ by diverse and varying combinations of maneuvers.

TEAM-dance seeks to avoid:
✔ trick movements done for their own sake;
✔ exaggerated grandstanding;
✔ movements that are unnatural or are harmful to the dog;
✔ movements that make the dog mimic a human rather than expressing its canine nature.

Following the Tradition of Dance

Out of these fundamental principles arose a form of dance that includes all the elements of classical dance, such as the use of space, basic positions, and directions of movement. Basic choreographic possibilities for dance partners were also adopted.

Right from the start, this presented a number of challenges:
✔ Conventional canine obedience systems are based on defined, stereotypical movements, while the tradition of dance calls for variability at every moment. Are dogs capable of accomplishing this enormous task?
✔ Dogs have often mastered many more movements than were required in the past. This almost unbelievable increase in the level of accomplishment can be attributed to a training system that combines integral motivation, diversity, constant attention, friendly communication, and a positive atmosphere.

✔ The dog will always be watching the hand holding the motivational object, regardless of where the hand moves or why. Naturally, this detracts from the overall impression and reduces the movements of the handler to a caricature of dance.

Movements of the Dance

The dog will be able to dance with the human within the limits of its abilities. This means that the dance must be designed and developed with these abilities in mind.

This enhanced adaptation is not a rational act in the sense of a human achievement, but as learned behavior it ranks as a considerable creative and intelligent accomplishment.

The Challenge of Verbal Cues

The great number of audible cues, together with the deliberate use of movement patterns that are not automatic, gave rise to a new challenge: During distance work, in the midst of moves that must be made in rapid succession, or at times of heightened anticipation, dogs often have trouble telling the difference between signals that sound alike. Each movement in dance requires different and new adaptations, and dogs use new strategies to master these. They no longer orient their responses totally to audible cues, but look for signals, including visible cues, that occur even before the audible cues.

As a result, even as the first audible signals begin to sound, the dog attempts to establish a link with the behavior pattern that appears most likely at that time. In the beginning, TEAM-dance was plagued by such confusion. The remedy was to develop new verbal cues, which are described later in this book.

Variosynchronous Pace

In the most highly developed form, both person and dog move exactly to the rhythm, with footfalls in unison. At the same time, their positions and their direction of movement are changing.

This type of dancing is called "vario"-synchronous pace because the passages danced in unison are continually

Even puppies learn what they can do through playful movement.

interspersed with asynchronous passages (solos). Also, in variosynchronous pace there are many variations in the pace itself.

For a detailed description, see the regulations for TEAM-dance which follow.

Freedom and Structure in the Dance

Dance has always stood at the focal point between freedom and structure. On the one hand, dance reflects the human desire to be restrained as little as possible by rules and regulations; in sports, on the other hand, rules promote equal opportunity and fair competition. Without rules, it would be impossible to compare one competitor with another. Furthermore, well-considered rules are not restrictive, but enriching and stimulating. Rules are indispensable in TEAM-dance as well, giving structure to dance as an athletic discipline and providing the dancers with a foundation for their creative artistry.

Contents of the TEAM-dance Regulations

✔ Embodiment of the TEAM concept and commitment to human–canine harmony.

✔ Protection of the dog against exploitation and unnatural requirements.

✔ Thoughtful consideration of the 15 principles of the Olympic Committee.

✔ Introductory information for novices.

✔ List of the basic dance possibilities.

Required Moves and Freestyle in TEAM-dance

TEAM-dance			
Technical Section (Compulsory)		**Artistic Section (Freestyle)**	
COMPONENTS	EVALUATION	COMPONENTS	EVALUATION ELEMENTS
Compulsory standards and elements	Pass or fail. – Points.	**a** Music	**A** Team harmony
		b Communication	**B** Artistic expression
Combinations of compulsory standards		**c** Compulsory standards	**C** Choreography: including logic of interpretation, order and transparency of form, richness of ideas, use of space
		c Advanced standards	
		d (Free, individual) creations	**D** Technical execution: including degree of difficulty, precision of rhythm and of movement

✔ Basis for athletic competition (comparison of performances).
✔ Definitions and requirements for performance levels.
✔ Establishment of minimum requirements.
✔ Fundamental principles for trials and tournaments.

TEAM-balance as Preparation

The TEAM-dance regulations also stipulate that before a team can enter a trial or a tournament, it must have completed the preliminary stage of TEAM-balance. This rule is intended to protect the dogs.
✔ Because TEAM-dance is based on the dog's free cooperation, a solid base of training and communication is essential.
✔ Simply redefining the areas of training and play has been known to cause numerous problems for dog owners. The endeavor to train and raise the dog with the help of dance, so to speak, brings a whole new circle of challenges.

For this reason, it is beneficial to form a solid basis in the preliminary stage of TEAM-balance before moving on to dance. Also, in order to participate in a trial, the dog must be at least 8 months old.

Compulsory Section

As in the sport of ice dancing, each TEAM-dance performance level has a corresponding section of required moves. The technical section (compulsory) and the artistic section (freestyle) are performed and evaluated separately in TEAM-dance. The team must complete the compulsory section successfully before it is allowed to perform the freestyle section.

Purpose of compulsory section:
✔ It establishes the overall performance level in the dance.
✔ It provides the basic framework of possible moves for the dance at each competition level. This guarantees that the freestyle presentations will remain comparable despite their individual diversity.
✔ Because it is relatively short, it is not too demanding in difficulty. The required moves simply ensure that the expected standard of performance will be met in each competition level.

Much of the TEAM-dance standards (compulsory section) is identical with the TEAM-sport standards. This link yields many advantages. Whether the handler eventually chooses to pursue sport or dance or both, the time spent working toward meeting the standards will have been beneficial to the team. Beginning at Level 3, of course, the standards for each of the two disciplines become more specialized.

For trials, the requirements in the compulsory section are uniform throughout. In tournaments, they are compiled anew by the judge for each competition.

Freestyle Section

In addition to a minimum of compulsory standards, extended standards must be demonstrated. The individually open portion of the freestyle section is taken up by so-called creations ("free elements"). However, the freestyle and individual creations may not include standards from higher competition levels.

In the evaluation of freestyle moves, "expression takes precedence over difficulty." It is not the more difficult individual moves that yield more points, but rather the presentation that shows technical mastery and convincing artistic expression.

Unfortunately, no evaluation of artistic merit is without a subjective component. To minimize the impact of this factor, TEAM-dance competitions always have several judges.

The Working Ring Space
✔ The official working ring for trials and tournaments for single and double teams is 42 × 56 feet (13 × 17 m). The long side faces the public. For outdoor events, depending on the locality, spectators may be seated along one, two, or three sides, allowing them to experience TEAM-dance from close at hand. A buffer zone 13 to 16 feet (4–5 m) wide protects the dance team from distractions or disturbances.

The TEAM-dance leader uses his entire body for artistic expression. That means no motivational objects—the dog is guided only by verbal cues.

TIP

Eligibility Requirements

✔ TEAM-dance is suitable for dogs of all breeds. Because you choose the music and the style of dance, your choreography can be adapted to your dog's breed and individual strengths.

✔ To enter trials at level 1, the dog must be at least 14 months old. At least 6 months must be spent at level 1 and again at level 2; the dog must stay at level 3 for 12 months before advancing to level 4.

✔ Dogs may compete at the same level for a maximum of two years. After that time, they may perform and receive comments from the judges, but the performance will not be scored. Thus, teams that for one reason or another are unable to advance, or choose not to advance, can still participate actively on a level that is appropriate for them.

✔ In formation dances (with three or more teams or five or more performers), the ring is enlarged to 52 × 66 feet (16 × 20 m). There are no fixed requirements for the structure of formations; for example, two human–canine teams and one solo dancer may perform in formation.

For training sessions, the working space can be much smaller.

The ring is divided into eight directions, which are numbered clockwise from 1 to 8 (with the main audience at center front) on clearly legible placards.

✔ In the compulsory section, the placards help to communicate the required move.

✔ In training sessions, they help the dancers orient themselves in the ring.

✔ In trials and in tournaments, they allow the judges and audience to comprehend the use of space in a choreography.

In presentations, care should be taken that:

✔ the music can be heard equally well everywhere in the ring;

✔ the available space is optimally used to promote artistic expression and choreographic logic.

The Music

The only stipulation is the length of the musical piece. This increases from one performance level to the next:

✔ level 1 lasts 1 to 2 minutes,

✔ level 2 lasts 1.5 to 2.5 minutes,

✔ level 3 lasts 2.5 to 4.5 minutes,

✔ level 4 lasts 2.5 to 6 minutes,

✔ the senior level lasts 2 to 4.5 minutes.

There is no advantage in regard to points for a longer piece.

The choice of music is practically unlimited; the handler can choose from any conceivable music and style, selecting music that is suitable for the particular dog and team.

Medleys are not permitted, because:

✔ "Cutting and pasting" different compositions detracts from the musical coherence.

✔ The music should not be used to fit in as many different gaits and individual exercises as possible, but rather should be interpreted in movement.

✔ Stringing together different rhythms or tempos often betrays a lack of skill in translating music into dance or bears witness to an impoverished understanding of art, which equates grandstanding and acrobatics with choreography and athleticism.

Note how both dance partners express their affection in this figure.

TEAM-dance does not set any requirements regarding the interpretation of the music (the choreography). The musical aspects of melody, rhythm, tone, form, and text, which are interwoven in the musical work of art, must be utilized. The choreographer must either recognize these intuitively or analyze them, bringing them to life in a new form. There are no limits to fantasy or creativity. It is left up to the individual to decide whether to emphasize the music's rhythm, melody, or theme, and whether to express it as serious, playful, nostalgic, or simply full of the joy of living. However, if the handler embarks upon a solo that the dog is unable to execute, the performance does not meet the primary criterion for evaluation—team harmony. This will be penalized heavily in the scoring.

Communication and Motivation

Because in TEAM-dance the entire body must be available for artistic expression, a problem arises: how to motivate the dog. Solving this problem calls upon all the knowledge and skills from the preliminary phase of TEAM-balance, during which both team partners learn to communicate and play meaningfully with each other. The dog has also learned to wait with concentration and commitment. Dance presents the same challenges, to a greater degree. The handler must not only communicate praise to the dog, but also make the matter so interesting that the dog never takes its eyes from the handler.

Some ways to do this:

✔ stimulating movements;

✔ a positive mood (conveyed by handler and music);

✔ reinforcement of desired behavior with verbal praise and play as reward;

✔ unpredictably interwoven games;

✔ canine communication signals.

Concrete exercises are communicated by verbal cues (see page 30). Because only these allow the handler freedom of movement for the dance, they should be used even if it is more difficult for the dog to follow them. In fact, by learning to distinguish many different verbal cues, the dog becomes more adept at taking in the wide range of acoustic communication from the handler. Once again, the prerequisite is a sustained positive mood. The dog awaits audible signals eagerly and even watches the handler's lips, because at every moment during the dance there are new exercises, communicated verbally.

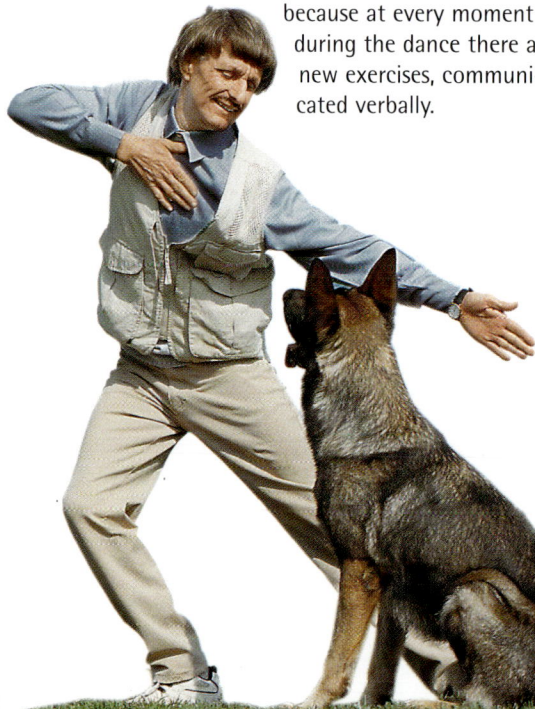

Standards, Elements, and Creations

So that the overall picture is not lost in mere individual exercises (elements), and to provide uniform structures for training and evaluation, TEAM-dance has been built up and organized according to distinct principles.

The "presentation material" is composed of standards, elements, and creations.

✔ Standards are defined in TEAM-dance according to various categories, such as positions, gaits, directions, figures, or tasks (such as coming closer or moving away, or motion and waiting).

For example: In the first standard (see page 32), the "basic positions" are listed. They describe how the two dance partners stand, sit, or lie in relation to each other (as if seen from above).

✔ Elements are self-contained tasks; they are subordinate to the standards.

For example: The parallel positions "Left" and "Right" are elements of the first standard within the positions (see table, page 32). For emphasis and greater distinctiveness, these elements were assigned relatively long signals (in comparison to other TEAM-dance signals).

✔ Creations are often derived from standards and elements. They can be used to broaden the team's repertoire and to enhance the individuality of the performance. An extensive description of the performance, the descriptive

Poses and steps alternate with figures executed by the partners together.

terms, and the corresponding verbal cues is published in the TEAM-dance regulations (see page 23) and in the training manual for TEAM-dance, now in preparation. The table on pages 32 to 34 gives a simplified overview.

As the dog begins its approach, a verbal cue tells whether it should leap over its partner or scoot under her.

Visible Signals and Verbal Cues

Visible signals are permitted in TEAM-dance levels 1 and 2, but points are deducted. They are not allowed in levels 3 and 4.

The table on pages 32 to 34 indicates the abundance of TEAM-dance verbal cues—some 30 cues for the elements in the basic form alone (compared to only nine cues in traditional obedience competitions). When inflections are added, there can easily be 70 signals in TEAM-dance; taking into account the various combinations and fine distinctions, in level 4 there are more than 100 cues.

Many will ask whether the dog can handle this. During the development of TEAM-dance, it was found that dogs can master the challenge—actively and joyfully. Even the variosynchronous pace (see pages 23 and 59) can be reliably guided with verbal cues in each individual step and in every tempo.

With utmost concentration and full anticipation, the dog seeks eye contact with the handler.

To facilitate mastery of the verbal cues and their uses, a compendium of cues for TEAM-dance was developed. This pioneering work may well change the way dogs are trained, far beyond the boundaries of dance. This is because the carefully directed use of verbal cues, and the dog's ability to master them, is certainly a new challenge in canine sports. And in dance, there is also the choreography to consider. In practice, it has been found that it's essential to give the dog time. Certain tasks, such as the variosynchronous pace or the many circles, pirouettes, and turns, cannot be mastered immediately—and excessive persistence in training is of no help.

Working with TEAM-dance Verbal Cues

✔ With few exceptions, the elements in TEAM-dance are defined in relation to the dog. Accordingly, "Left" means that the dog is on the left of the handler; "taw" (sometimes "ta") or "tee" indicates how the dog is to step.

✔ All cues are given relative to the dog's movement. In the example "in front position, dog moves forward, handler backward," the

handler must cue the dog "taw" to step with its left foreleg; at the same time, the handler steps back with the right leg.

✔ The problem of timing: The handler knows well in advance which element is coming next; the dog does not. The dog must rely on verbal cues, which often come too late. It's unreasonable to expect the dog to execute a move at the same instant that the cue is heard. Obviously, the cues must be given in good time. For the especially important phases of starting and stopping, therefore, the cue is preceded by an advance cue. For example, "Go – taw" means "ready, move forward, starting on the left foreleg."

✔ For many exercises, a single cue is not

Hearing a soft, friendly "Down," the dog drops to the ground, without interrupting the communication for even an instant.

enough. For example, if a dog (in TEAM-dance level 4) is to move backwards, starting with the left foreleg, then the cues "Back" and "taw" are given in succession, again in plenty of time.

✔ The dog hears the verbal cue, but also sees it, because he is watching the movements of the handler's mouth and the rise and fall of the chest wall. This was taken into consideration as the cues were developed.

TEAM-dance Compendium: Standards, Elements, and Cues

Standards	Elements (Compulsory and Additional Moves)	Cues
1 Basic positions	1a) Parallel position, left 1b) Parallel position, right 2) Front position 3) In line (D in front of P, D behind P)	"Left" "Right" "Front" "Before" or "Behind"
2 Basic postures	1) Stand 2) Sit 3) Down	"Stand" "Sit" "Down"
3 Changes of position	1a) Parallel from left to right 1b) Parallel from right to left 2a) From front to parallel left 2b) From front to parallel right 3a) From parallel left to front 3b) From parallel right to front x) From any other position to parallel left or right y) From any other position to front	"ree" "law" "Left" "Right" "Front" "Front" "Left" or "Right" "Front"
4 Changes of posture	1a) From standing to sitting 1b) From standing to lying down 2a) From sitting to standing 2b) From sitting to lying down 3a) From lying down to sitting 3b) From lying down to standing	"Sit" "Down" "Stand" "Down" "Sit" "Stand"
5 (Variable) Approach	1a) Front position standing (D comes from nearby to P, faces H exactly centered, stands) 2a) Approach from medium or long distance, followed by standing 2b) Approach from medium or long distance, followed by sitting 2c) Approach from medium or long distance, followed by lying down 3a) From any position to in-line positions (D stands, sits, or lies down in front of H in line) 3b) From any position to in-line positions (D stands, sits, or lies down behind H in line)	"Front" "Come–Stand" "Come–Sit" "Come–Down" "Before" "Behind"
6 (Variable) Move Away	1a) Move away a short distance (2 to 3 steps) 1b) Move away a medium distance (4 to 8 steps) 1c) Move away a long distance (more than 8 steps)	"Away"
7 Action and Waiting (P and/or D)	1) D active phase 2a) D brief waiting phase (1 to 2 seconds) 2b) D medium waiting phase (3 to 4 seconds) 2c) D long waiting phase (more than 4 seconds)	Appropriate cues and pauses

D = dog, H = handler; x and y represent any other positions.

TEAM-dance Compendium: Standards, Elements, and Cues

Standards	Elements (Compulsory and Additional Moves)	Cues
8 Proximity and distance	1) Proximity (positions) 2) Short distance (about 2 to 3 steps) 3) Medium distance (about 4 to 8 steps) 4) Long distance (more than 8 steps)	As before
9 Starting and stopping	Starting Stopping	"Go–taw" or "Go–tee" With no advance cue: "Stop" or "Stand" With advance cue: "Halt–Stop"
10 Primary directions (forward, backward, lateral, diagonal)	1a) Forward in front position 1b) Forward in parallel position 1c) Forward in in-line position 2) D approaches (standing) H (front position) 3a), b), c) Backward together: H and D in the same direction (in each of the basic positions) 4) Approaching each other (front position) from a distance 5) Moving apart (H and D in opposite directions) 6) Backward solo (D alone, H pause or solo) 7) Lateral 8) Diagonal	"Go" or "Forward" "Go" "Go" "Go" "Back" "Go" "Part" "Part" "Tra–va" and "Tra–vee" "Tra–va" and "Tra–vee"
11 Gaits	1) Walk 2) Trot 3) Gallop	"Walk" with "taw" or "tee" "Trot" with "taw" or "tee" "Gallop" (without VSP)
12 Paces/Tempos	1) 2/2, 3/4, and 4/4 time (and other beats) 2) Spanish walk 3) Alla breve (quick time) 4) Traverse in front and parallel position 5) Triplet step 6) Quadruplet step x) Additional meters	"taw" "tee" or "tee" "taw" "ta-ha" "te-hee" "taw" "tee" + frequency and pitch "Tra–va" "Tra–vee" "ta-tee-ta" on 1 basic beat "ta-tee ta-tee" on 3–group
13 (Simple) figures	1) Straight line; 2) curve; 3) serpentine; 4) square; 5) rectangle; 6) triangle; 7) circle; 8) figure 8 (See the corresponding standards.)	As needed, cues for turns and circles
14 Turns, pivots, circle turns, head turns	1a) Turn left, 90 degrees (D) 1b) Turn right, 90 degrees (D) 2a) Pivot (180-degree turn) together, left and right (H and D in parallel position turning in the same direction)	"haw" "gee" "kaw" "kee"

TEAM-dance Compendium: Standards, Elements, and Cues

Standards	Elements (Compulsory and Additional Moves)	Cues
14 Turns, pivots, circle turns, head turns	2b) Pivot (180-degree turn), opposite directions, left and right (H and D in parallel position, turn in opposite directions)	"kaw" "kee"
	3a), b) H counter-clockwise turn left (right position) and right (left position)	"haw" "gee"
	4a), b) D counter-clockwise turn left (right position) and right (left position)	"kaw" "kee"
	5a), b) Head turn left and right	"shaw" "shee"
15 Circles and ring-arounds	1a) + b) Circle together 360° (x times), left and right positions	May be done with or without cues
	2a) + b) Partial circles (180°, 270°) together, left and right positions	"kaw" "kee"
	3a) + b) Circle opposite directions 360° (x times), left and right positions	"kaw" "kee"
	4a) + b) Partial circles (270°), opposite directions, left and right positions	"kaw" "kee"
	5x) Backward circles and partial circles in left and right positions	"Back"
	6x) Ring-arounds (H in pose, move, or figure)	"Ring-aw" and "Ring-ec"
16 Pirouettes and circles	1x) Solo pirouette 360° (x times), left and right, near and at a distance, simultaneous and delayed. In left position, turning left; in right position, turning right.	"Twist-aw" or "Twist-ee"
	2x) Team pirouettes: Same direction, simultaneous and delayed, turning left and right.	"Twist-aw" or "Twist-ee"
	3x) Team pirouettes: Opposite directions, in left or right position, simultaneous and delayed.	"kaw" or "kee"
	4 x) Frontal circle.	"zaw" or "zee"
	5 x) Foreleg circle (left position clockwise = +, counterclockwise = –) and (right position...) Circle in right position clockwise = +, counterclockwise = –; mirror image in left position.	"zaw" or "zee"
	6 x) The corresponding hind leg circles.	"zaw" or "zee"
17 Floor figures	1a and b) Lying on left side and on right side.	"Lie-haw" or "Lie-gee"
	2a and b) Rolling over to left and right (D).	"Roll-haw" or "Roll-gee"
	3a) Crawling forward and similar moves.	
18 Leaps	x) As desired, over (or through) arm, knee, upper body (signals for approach and leap).	"Start–Jump"
	x) Run underneath (as opposed to jumping over).	"Start–Under"
19 Variosynchronous pace (VSP)	x) In each tempo and in all gaits.	"taw," "tee," "ta-ha," "te-hee," "ho," by pitch, crescendo, and timing of cues

D = dog, H = handler; x and y represent any other positions.

Working with Verbal Cues

The verbal cues developed for TEAM-dance are meaningful combinations of syllables that make it easier for the dog to decode the signals.

✔ The TEAM-dance compendium of verbal cues, of course, was originally developed in German by Ekard Lind. It has been adapted here for English-speaking handlers.

✔ The vowel sound "aw" indicates all movements or positions that go to the left, and the sound "ee" indicates those that go to the right.

✔ The sounds "taw" and "tee" (or, in quick time, "ta" and "ti") stand for steps with the dog's left and right foreleg.

✔ "Left" and "Right" signal the basic positions on the left and right side of the handler.

✔ The syllables "law" and "ree" are cues for the "flying side change" while moving forward.

✔ The cues "zaw" and "zee" introduce circle figures.

✔ Many signals, such as "Down" and "Stand," are familiar from traditional obedience commands. In TEAM-dance, however, the dog must learn to recognize all possible combinations of the positions.

✔ Individual handlers are allowed to decide which signals to use in TEAM-dance; they may either choose from the compendium or use their own words. However, because judges use the recommended TEAM-dance signals in the compulsory section, the handler must at least be familiar with them.

✔ If a team has trouble using any of the recommended cues, the handler should by all means take the initiative of inventing new signals that are easier for the dog to recognize.

✔ The widely used command "Heel" is not used at all, because it cannot adequately describe the complex variety of possible tasks, such as walking at the handler's left or right, in front of or behind the handler, approaching the handler at a certain tempo, and stopping at a precise time.

✔ For the reasons described above, there is a separate verbal cue for almost every task in TEAM-dance.

Circles, turns, and pirouettes can be combined into hundreds of variations.

Levels, Classes, Sections

TEAM-dance incorporates four performance levels, increasing in degree of difficulty. The difference arises from the introduction of new, more complex, and technically more demanding elements and combinations. In the fifth and final level, the senior level, the challenges are reduced again.

A particular freestyle presentation need not include all 19 standards, because the team has already demonstrated in the compulsory section that it meets the performance standard. In fact, it is advisable not to include all the standards in a single piece, but rather to demonstrate the standards while emphasizing artistic interpretation and expression. This recommendation also serves to encourage variety in the freestyle presentations. It's better not to repeat the same elements over and over in every piece.

TEAM-dance Sections

TEAM-dance is divided into five sections and three classes (see figure).

✔ TEAM-dance *Classic* is the main section. Here, every measure can be choreographed and practiced until it is technically perfect.

TFAM-dance-Divisions

TEAM-dance Classes

A TEAM-dance Pairs

B (Small) TEAM-dance Formations (up to 5 participants)

C (Large) TEAM-dance Formations (6 or more participants)

TEAM-dance Sections

1 TEAM-dance Classic

2 TEAM-dance Improvisation

3 TEAM-dance Standard Dances

4 TEAM-dance Program

5 TEAM-dance Open

TEAM-dance Categories

1 TEAM-score (Team evaluation)

2 TEAM-partner score (Focus: the dog's performance)

3 TEAM-leader score (Focus: the handler)

✔ In TEAM-dance *Improvisation*, the participants do not know in advance what the music will be. They must develop their presentation with the dog extemporaneously.

✔ TEAM-dance *Standard Dances* follows the model of traditional dances.

✔ TEAM-dance *Program*, the theme dance, is a particularly interesting section, because

When puppies tussle over a toy, it's often more about playful socialization than about who ends up with the prize.

the organizer of a competition can prescribe a particular theme—perhaps a particular style or piece of music, or a certain musical group, composer, or motto—which each pair interprets individually. Such theme presentations offer the audience interesting opportunities for comparison.

✔ In TEAM-dance *Open,* anything goes. This allows ample room for those with avant-garde tastes or a talent for experimentation to exercise their imaginations. Acrobatic presentations also are appropriate here.

Under discussion is a sixth TEAM-dance section, a *Masters* section, which would require a high level of dancing ability on the part of the handler.

Categories

For scoring, TEAM-dance is divided into three categories (see page 36). This permits the team leader to adapt the dance to the team's needs and capabilities. For example, a handler who does not wish to do much dancing, perhaps taking only simple steps, could choose not to enter the team in Category 3.

Standards for Evaluation

These are the descriptions of the qualitative and formal elements of performance, as set forth in the rules for trials. The maximum score is 100 points (see figure, page 40), with a possible 20 points each for the compulsory section, team harmony, artistic expression, choreography, and technical execution. This allocation reflects the emphasis on artistic merit, with 60 points for qualitative elements and 40 points for formal elements (compulsory section plus technical execution).

The points are awarded according to the following evaluation scale:
✔ 16–20 points for a grade of "very good";

Every TEAM-dance presentation begins with the official TEAM-dance salute.

✔ 11–15 points for a grade of "good";
✔ 6–10 points for a grade of "satisfactory"; and
✔ 0–5 points for a grade of "unsatisfactory."

A grade of 6 points or more is considered a passing grade.

The compulsory section, team harmony, artistic expression, choreography, and technical execution are further broken down into detailed evaluation criteria, which are described in the rules for trials.

Checklist
Principles for Evaluation

1 Harmony: The TEAM-dance presentation should present a self-contained unit.

2 Preparation, training, practice, trials, and tournaments are to be structured in such a way as to serve the goal of human–canine harmony.

3 TEAM concept: The needs of human and dog should be met in a way that is ethically justifiable for both.

4 Figures that emphasize the canine athlete and steps executed by the team together should be choreographically linked and balanced. Excessive demands are to be avoided.

5 Artistic–athletic achievement: Participants in TEAM-dance commit to this ideal, following the model of the Olympic principles.

6 Artistic expression is valued more highly than acrobatic stunts and isolated technical perfection.

7 TEAM-dance salute (see photo, page 37): In this salute, the leader expresses consent to these principles for evaluation.

Handler Awards, Partner Awards

In addition to evaluating the team performance, the judges may recognize the performance of an individual leader (as trainer and dancer) or a four-legged competitor with one additional grade each.

Thus, for example, an award might be given to a handler who has difficulty performing in public but clearly did exceptional work as a trainer, or to a handler who has little experience in training a TEAM-dance dog but gave an outstanding performance as a dancer.

However, these special awards may be given only if the team has met the basic principles for evaluation (see checklist at left). Isolated one-sided accomplishments that do not meet the criterion of harmony are not compatible with the TEAM concept.

In addition, the organizers may award other prizes, such as for the best choreography.

Each team is evaluated by at least two judges. The organizers may also appoint other members to the panel of judges, who may represent the fields of music, dance, athletics, journalism, dog breeding, or research.

Unmistakably TEAM-dance

TEAM-dance was developed after the model of ballroom dancing competitions. The rules serve on the one hand to protect the dog against unnatural or imitative positions, and on the other hand to lay the foundation for a challenging, athletic, artistic, and aesthetically pleasing performance. The TEAM concept was formulated on the basis of human–canine harmony, athletic ideals, and artistic goals. It finds expression in the rules and in the structure of the standards, elements, and creations. Of all the ways that humans and dogs can interact in motion, simply moving together in a common step is eminently suited to expressing

Pose (the handler) and change of position (the canine dance partner).

the team concept in the sense of a shared athletic and artistic presentation. For this reason, steps and figures are of equal value in TEAM-dance.

A special feature of TEAM-dance is the vario-synchronous pace (see pages 23, 59) as the expression of a highly cultivated team rapport.

The Senior Level

By offering a senior level, TEAM-dance for the first time in the history of canine competition created a platform for challenging performances even by dogs who are no longer in the prime of life. Dogs who have reached 75 percent of the life expectancy for their breed or who are demonstrably limited in physical ability or health are permitted (though not required) to compete at the senior level.

Most Schutzhund* dogs are trained for about three years, then shown for three to four years. When the dog is six to eight years old, its chances of winning are so low that its owner no longer enjoys showing it. What happens next is all too familiar: The dog is sold, given

*The German term *Schutzhund* refers to a dog that has completed a multifaceted training regimen including obedience and protection work. The term is used and understood universally.

A Guide to Scoring

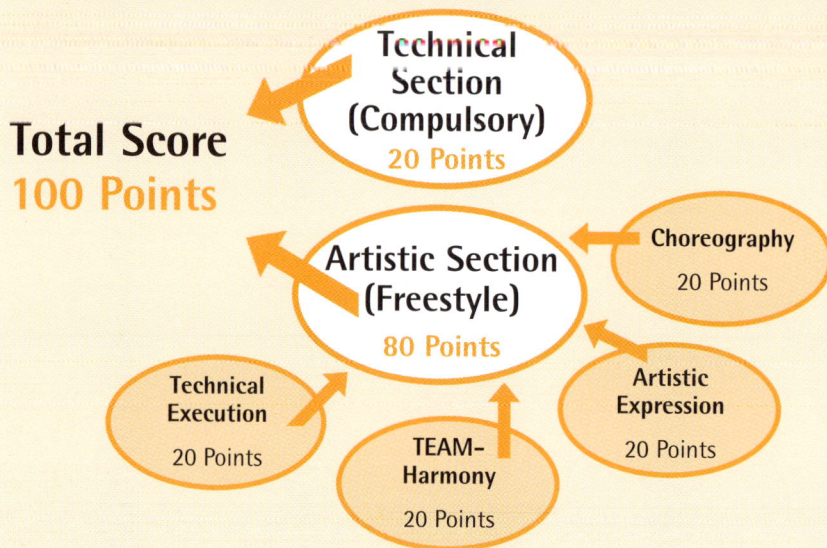

Total Score
100 Points

Technical Section (Compulsory)
20 Points

Artistic Section (Freestyle)
80 Points

Choreography
20 Points

Technical Execution
20 Points

TEAM-Harmony
20 Points

Artistic Expression
20 Points

away, put to sleep, or simply retired. And yet many dogs at age six to eight are still quite capable of presenting wonderful dance performances. It could even be said that in this discipline, where the bond between human and canine is so important, more can be expected of older dogs than of younger dogs. Leaps are prohibited at the senior level, however, as are other movements that are clearly beyond the individual dog's ability. The senior level is also a boon to the handler, who—after investing so much time and energy in training the dog—can still enjoy another three to five years of performing with the same partner and need not yet start working with a second dog.

Qualitative and Formal Performance

These requirements take seriously the age-old ideal of the "happy dog." Of course, lip service has always been paid to this dream, but only too often even its well-intentioned pursuit falls short of the goal.

The Compendium of Verbal Cues

In TEAM-dance, the dog is guided by an extensive system of verbal cues. The system, developed by Ekard Lind, takes into account the ease of recognition, intentional similarity, and distinctive differences of the acoustic signals, as well as the visible signal elements of the spoken words and sounds (movements of lips and cheeks, rise and fall of the chest wall). The verbal cues are summarized in a comprehensive listing (the TEAM-dance Compendium).

Motivational Objects

Motivational objects may be carried during performances, as long as they remain out of sight. At the end of the presentation, the handler may show, toss, or otherwise offer the motivational object. To prevent rambunctious behavior, the handler must leave the working ring within six seconds.

Test Appearances

Following the equestrian model, in TEAM-dance and TEAM-sport there is the possibility of entering a trial for a test appearance that is not evaluated. This may be done three times a year. The purpose is to gain experience in performing in public, while making sure that the dog does not associate any negative experiences with the performance. This test appearance may include an interlude of free play, not to exceed eight seconds, so that the dog does not gain the frustrating impression that trials or tournaments are not fun.

Repeating an Exercise

If a dog makes a mistake in an exercise during a trial or in TEAM-sport, the handler may simply raise a hand, then repeat that exercise up to two times, with noncoercive aids allowed. This corrective section receives a score of 0. The advantage is that the dog does not leave the ring with the impression that the mistake was acceptable.

TEAM-dance and Health Issues

Physicians and veterinarians consider TEAM-dance to be a very healthful form of sport. Even older dogs or those with physical limitations can participate, often with amazing success. To protect the dogs, TEAM-dance judges are instructed to warn the handlers of obviously sick or over-challenged dogs, and in extreme cases they may eliminate the team from competition. A physical examination certifying that the dog can participate in the sport is recommended but not required.

Rule Revisions

The existing rules are not carved in stone and institutionalized; rather, they may be adapted to the needs of a rapidly changing society. For this reason, the rules for TEAM-dance and TEAM-sport include provisions for revisions. Every two years, a conference of the TWZ takes place, at which changes in the rules are discussed and implemented as necessary. This committee comprises TEAM-dance specialists from all the fields involved: judges, competitors, trainers, veterinarians, and organizers. The committee may also consult musicians, dancers, choreographers, composers, editors, publishers, media representatives, and others.

This dog is not just standing on its hind legs— such mimicry is frowned upon in TEAM-dance. Rather, the team is taking off in a tandem leap.

ENJOYING THE DISCIPLINE OF TEAM-DANCE

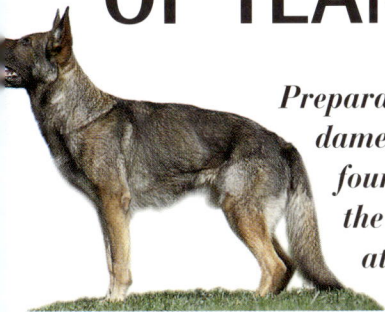

Preparation, in the form of play and motivation, is fundamental to the enjoyment of dance. The better the foundation established in TEAM-balance, the easier the transition to TEAM-dance. You'll be surprised at how dramatically music enhances the way you already enjoy playing with your dog.

Procedural Requirements

To enter TEAM-dance trials and tournaments, the team leader must present the following documents:
✔ photo ID
✔ immunization record
✔ proof of liability insurance
✔ identity papers (genealogy or additional registration)
✔ proof that dog meets age requirement (see page 26)
✔ performance record
✔ TEAM-dance salute (see pages 37, 49).

Practical Requirements

Right from the start, it can be a challenge to maintain the right balance of training, communication, play, motivation, and possibly also specialized tasks. For this reason, I suggest taking up dance only after the fundamentals of training are established and after any

specialized tasks are mastered. Of course, this does not mean that you couldn't include dance now and then, carefully interwoven.

It is necessary, however, that the dog has been trained as thoroughly as possible. For puppies, the goals of socialization (to humans and to other dogs), building trust, training, and the offering of developmental stimuli and training opportunities take absolute precedence. The dog should have enjoyed a modern puppy play course and then completed a few months of TEAM-balance.

The person who has plenty of time and also the necessary knowledge and skills, however, will surely want to take advantage of puppyhood as the dog's most valuable learning years, in dance as well.
✔ Development of "syntonic" (sensitive) communication with the dog—that is, establishing a bond with the dog.
✔ Motivating the dog, and at the same time holding it in check with hands-off restraints (in the form of recognized authority).
✔ Development of "integral motivation" on the basis of canine behavior. Motivation is not merely reward for a completed task, but rather should arise out of joy in the task itself.

TEAM-dance at its best: The leader in an arabesque, the partner in mid-leap. The dog moves exactly in time with the beat of the music.

Checklist
Equipment Needs

1 Sound system: This can be a cassette player, CD player, or mini-disk player. The latter is especially well suited for dance because each musical piece can be readily taken apart into as many segments as you like, and then put back together. Each individual segment can be repeated in a loop as often as needed for practice sessions.

2 Portable player: Small enough to fit in a waist pack or pocket, with headphones. (A system designed for jogging works best.)

3 Metronome: This marks time with a certain number of beats per minute. Most modern versions are electronic. Choose a metronome that will display the number of beats per minute digitally when you press a button. This will let you know right away whether the piece of music in question has the right tempo.

✔ Development of "sustained motivation" by carefully directed cultivation of play, until the dog is not distracted by anything else.
✔ Building a solid foundation, then setting clear priorities. Without sound and stable priorities, athletic activities are not promising in the long run.

It takes a good deal of sensitivity and perceptiveness to keep the whole picture in balance at all times.

Where to Practice?

You can practice TEAM-dance almost anywhere—in your house, garage, or yard; in a country meadow, in a city park, or on the beach; in an empty parking lot or parking garage; and of course at a dog training area or in a riding arena.

Some people will have space to set up their own working ring, with dimensions of 42 × 56 feet (13 × 17 m). If necessary, you can make do with 39 × 53 feet (12 × 16 m).

When you are practicing without a dog, you can also use a gymnasium, school hall, or other indoor space.

How to Practice?
The most important tips are these:
✔ The handler must be very familiar with the piece and have learned the steps thoroughly before bringing the dog into the act.
✔ The dog must never, under any circumstances, be overworked. Check carefully to be sure that you have broken down the learning process into sufficiently small steps. If the dog cannot keep up, it's better to drop back two or three steps or to insert an intermediate lesson.
✔ Create a positive learning atmosphere. Impatience and anger, or lack of interest, reduce your chances of success.
✔ Use plenty of body language at the start, then gradually less and less.

How Long to Practice?

Here there are no rules, for each dog reacts differently. As a rule of thumb: You should watch the dog carefully, and stop at the first sign of diminishing concentration or waning motivation. If sustaining motivation for even a short time is difficult, it may be that this TEAM is out of balance. In that case, it would be advisable to review the fundamentals of TEAM-balance under the guidance of an experienced trainer until the foundation is solid.

What Else Is Needed?

✔ Helpful aids include training corridors, consisting of posts and plastic mesh fencing, as well as two long switches for control from a distance.

Many dogs enjoy energetic play—the more diversity, the better.

✔ Whenever possible, you should try to do without a leash or lead line and guide the dog with body language, pantomime, gestures, and with motivation and authority. If you do not use a leash, you will not be tempted to compensate for your own awkwardness by tugging at the leash.

✔ The handler should have learned how to use all types of motivational objects and should be able to use all kinds of motivation when working with the dog.

BEHAVIOR GUIDE

The simple example of "releasing the prey" will show clearly that the dog is a creature with extremely complicated, overlapping, and at the same time also conflicting behavior patterns. Releasing the prey is at first unnatural. Even a puppy knows that prey must be guarded. Nevertheless, a dog can learn to release. Often, this involves a conflict between instinct and accommodation (adaptation).

1. A weaker dog can gain self-confidence in a playful tug-of-war, while a dog that tends to dominate must learn to accept its status and the rules of the game.

2. (Far left) For the game to be credible, the dog must be able to win. Right after it gains the prey, however, the dog's hunting instinct is still strong.

3. (Left) Because the prey is "dead" once the man has let go, the dog's hunting mood begins to subside. It will soon turn its attention to other stimuli—as in the photo; note how the dog's head has turned.

4. (Right) It would be a mistake at this point to try to grab the motivational object. The dog's instinct to guard the prey would flare up at once. In the photo, the dog's eyes show this change in attitude.

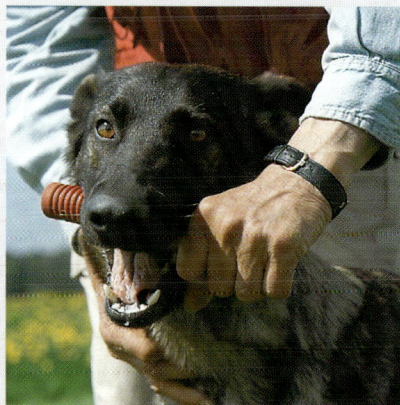

5. (Far right) Led by instinct, the dog would resist immediately and vigorously.

6. The correct approach is to watch and wait until the "hunting mood" has subsided, and then...

7. ...quietly and calmly, without speaking, take the motivational object. A forceful "Give" command would immediately revive the "hunting mood." After the object is released, a calm, relaxing "Give" may be spoken.

8. A genuine conflict situation: Because past experience has taught the dog that the motivational object will be returned immediately, he releases it. But his instincts say "Don't give it up!" The conflict is evident in his darting tongue and blazing eyes.

9. This uncomfortable conflict must not be prolonged or else the dog's instinctive behavior will be reinforced. As a result, the dog will very likely have problems releasing in the future.

10. For this reason, immediately after the spoken "Give," the handler should reactivate the motivational object by tossing it to the ground. The dog should learn to expect a favorable outcome to the conflict.

TIP

"Free Dancing" Without a Dog

To awaken and enhance your creativity, skill, and confidence in dancing with your dog, it's a good idea to practice without a dog. Freed of the responsibility for training your partner, you can move to the music as you please. For best results, find a place and time when nobody is watching.

Here's what to do:

✔ Swing into action: Put on your favorite music, and simply bob and sway to its rhythm until you feel comfortable and involved.

✔ Dance with free steps: After a while, start to move around, but keep on swaying to the music. Your whole body should be involved as you step and turn. Relax, enjoy yourself, and move in harmony with the music.

✔ If you like, you might hum or sing along. Do whatever helps you open yourself to dancing freely.

Off to a Good Start

When you're ready, it's time to invite your canine partner to join you.

1. Choose the same music you used when free-dancing. Do everything you can to make this first experience a success. If you can give your dog the same sense of enjoyment that you felt when dancing freely on your own, you will have taken a very important first step.

✔ At first, don't ask your dog to do anything specific. The dog should learn that music and dancing create a pleasurable bond with you.

✔ With movements, voice, gestures, and pantomime, stimulate the dog to move with the music. Don't dance with the dog at first—just watch.

✔ Reward and encourage the dog's movements with praise.

These first attempts may take several days or weeks, depending on the dog's level of concentration and motivation. It's not the length of the initial training period that counts, but rather the quality. The practice sessions themselves are better too short than too long.

2. If the dog responds well to music and to your stimulation, move on to musical free play. Here, the handler leads the play according to the music. For example, you might:

✔ face the dog and step forward and back in time to the music;

✔ turn in rhythmical circles as you play with the dog;

✔ raise or lower the intensity of your play as the music changes;

✔ pause and hold still, as a signal calling for attention, at a point when the instruments and voices are silent. When the music starts again, give another signal that triggers action and resume your free play.

It can take at least two weeks (usually longer!) to solidify this phase. You will notice that after a short time, just turning on the music is enough to put your dog in a positive mood.

3. As the spirit of playful harmony associated with the music grows, you can introduce more movements, changes of direction, and simple figures (such as circles), matching them to the rhythm and melody of the music. However, don't expect your dog to move in time with the music yet. Cultivate this "improvised dance." This form both demands and promotes spontaneity and creativity.

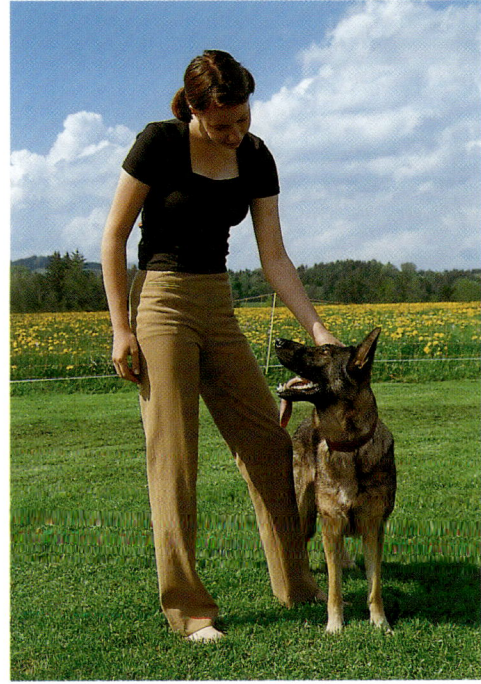

The TEAM-dance Salute and Free Play

The handler and dog enter the ring together. When they are ready to begin their performance, the handler presents the TEAM-dance salute, arms raised overhead and hands touching (see page 37). This is important for several reasons:

✔ It allows communication with the technician. When the judges give the signal that the team may start, and the sound system and music are ready, the technician raises a hand. When the handler ends the salute, arms down, the technician starts the music, which is introduced by another four or five seconds of silence. In the waiting phase, before the music begins to play, the dog should be in a posture of high concentration and happy anticipation.

Left: After the salute, and maintaining eye contact, the team begins to move.
Right: Each correctly performed exercise is rewarded.

This introductory routine permits the handler to decide exactly when to start, while still accommodating the needs of the technician and the judges.

✔ The salute has symbolic meaning. The circle formed by the upraised arms and touching hands represents the handler's commitment to:
• human–canine harmony;
• ethical responsibility; and
• the TEAM presentation in the spirit of sport.

Those who are not prepared to give the TEAM-dance salute are not allowed to participate.

Even a puppy can enjoy the first steps in the transition from play to dance.

✔ The salute provides an excellent introduction for dance training. After the handler has made all the necessary preparations—setting up the sound system, preparing the music, taking the dog out for a while, eliminating distractions—the team enters the ring together. Standing before the dog (who may be sitting, standing, or lying down), the handler gives the TEAM-dance salute and starts the music. During the waiting phase, appropriate body language and eye contact bring the dog to alert attention. It's important for the dog to demonstrate interest in the handler, rather than just staring fixedly at the vest pocket where the motivational object may be hidden. With the first beats of the music, the handler gives the accustomed signal and the free play begins.

After only a few days, the dog will respond happily even as the handler is preparing to give the TEAM-dance salute. Experienced TEAM-dancers continue this ritual even with dogs that have danced for several years and have mastered the movements of the highest performance level.

One Step at a Time

1. Now you are ready to introduce rhythmic and melodic elements that shape the play more and more to the music. In this way, the dog learns to incorporate its own natural movement patterns, without coercion or stress.

2. Then—and still in keeping with the music— introduce responses that the dog has already learned, such as "Sit," "Down," "Stop," "Come," or turning left or right.

Important reminders:

✔ Proceed very carefully!

✔ Watch the dog, maintaining contact and a positive mood.

✔ Don't ask too much at once!

✔ Keep going back to the relaxed "free dancing," and intersperse games that involve movement, affection, and of course edible treats and fetch-and-release.

If at some point during the dance you notice that the balance isn't right, you should try to correct the problem under everyday circumstances before you continue with the dance. For example, many dogs have difficulty holding still while the handler is moving actively about, possibly with expressive arm movements. It's a good idea to let the dog become accustomed to this gradually; start with only a few movements, adding more as the dog learns to hold still.

If your dog responds more and more clearly to rhythm and melody, and also will stay in a given posture when and for as long as you want, you have already made great progress. As soon as your dog has done what you want, either by moving or holding a posture, be prompt and generous with praise. This will reinforce the behavior.

Developing the Standards and Elements

The first training phase lasts about one to three months. Now you can begin to develop the repertoire described in the standards.

There are two ways to do this:

✔ Practicing with music from the start. This holistic method can be risky, however, because

The corridor as "passive reinforcement" makes it easier to learn a maneuver.

of the complexity of factors involved; it is not recommended, at least for novices.

✔ Practicing the elements without music. This method is simpler and safer. The elements are learned individually, without the constraints of music and choreography. It's best to begin with elements that are similar to movements the dog already knows or with exercises that you're sure the dog can do without difficulty.

Choreography

Choreography involves many intermediate steps—drafting, modifying, rejecting, refining. This is normal. It can also be frustrating to have to admit, time and again, that you have not yet found the best solution. A successfully choreographed routine, however, is a true work of art—timeless, unique, and fascinating.

Selecting Music

The music is one of the most important elements of dance. You must remember that the piece you choose will be with you for a long time, often for years, and that producing a choreographic work takes an enormous amount of time. Therefore, it's essential to use all conceivable care and foresight when selecting music. Before you decide on a piece, you should try dancing to it more than once, with and without your dog.

As a rule, it's a good idea to seek help from experts. These may be people who have studied music—music teachers, orchestra members, composers, or those who give lessons on the piano or other instruments. Especially sought after, of course, are choreographers and dance teachers, who offer not only their dancing ability but a wealth of knowledge and skills relating to music. Without expert assistance, dance often remains only an amateurish activity. A professional musician can readily provide the information you need for your initial analysis of a piece (see page 53), such as its tempo, beat, meter, rhythm, formal structure, and special features—all very important for dancing. There is much to be said for consulting a professional.

Ideas for the Dance

After much thought, you have decided on a piece of music. The next step is to gather ideas and material for the dance. Here too, you should take plenty of time—but don't let your imagination run wild. Anyone who has ever choreographed a dance knows that it often takes months, even years, to reach its final form. Ideas are drafted, revised, discarded, and reinvented as the choreographed work matures.

Therefore, it's a good idea to come up with a list of ideas and try several of them out. Only by experimenting will you know whether and how an idea works out in reality. The more critically

This floor figure is not difficult to execute, and it suits this dog.

you test your ideas, the less time and energy you will spend on mistakes.

Always keep in mind the question of feasibility. Ask yourself:

✔ Is this idea appropriate for me and my dog? Can the team perform the necessary moves?

✔ What direction should I take when seeking ideas? What appeals to me and to my dog? Does my dog like running? Leaping? Action-packed games, or gentle ones? Slow games, or fast ones?

✔ What is the central statement of the musical piece, and can I interpret this "theme" in dance with my dog?

✔ Where would I like to develop contrasts, or similarities, or repetitions?

Initial Analysis

First of all, you need information about the central artistic statement of the piece (its theme), as well as its tempo, beat, meter, rhythm, key (major or minor), overall formal structure, and special characteristics. Don't hesitate to ask an expert for assistance. This will help you not only to avoid major mistakes, but also to develop a considerably deeper understanding of the piece, leading to new inspirations and ideas for the dance.

Formal Analysis

Next, you will want to analyze how the piece is organized.

✔ Is it divided into parts? If so, how many? Is the form a–b–a or a–b–c?

✔ Does the piece have an introduction, or a passage (called a *coda*) that brings it to a formal close?

✔ Does the piece have transitions? In which measures?

✔ How many measures does the theme contain?

✔ Is there a secondary theme?

Checklist
Choosing Your Music

1 Character: The music must be pleasing, and it should be inspiring. It must stand the test of time. For this reason, you should consider its artistic merit.

2 Duration: It should not be much longer than the length stipulated for the intended performance level, unless it includes pauses at which you can fade it out.

3 Tempo: The pace of the music should be appropriate for your dog.

4 Difficulty: Novices should seek pieces with a strong, definite rhythm and a clear melody and structure.

5 Dance-ability: The music you choose should be well suited for you and for your dog.

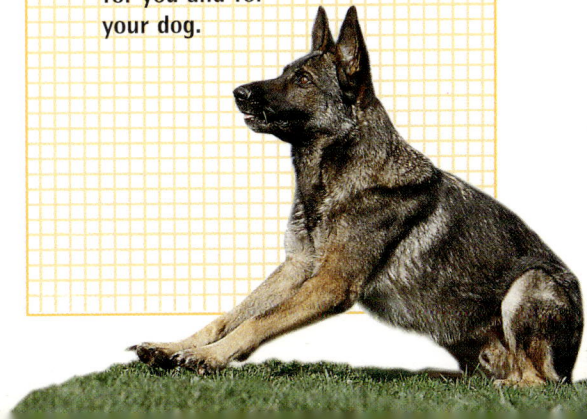

TIP

Memory Aids

As time goes by, it's all too easy to forget even the best ideas. Be sure to write down each experiment, each stage of your choreography, at least in key words, and save them in chronological order.

✔ Many find it useful to keep a file of all their choreographed pieces, numbered in order.

✔ The "choreocell" is a sketch of the performance as if seen from above, using symbols and words to describe the movements. It has the advantage that even a person with no particular musical knowledge can write and follow it. However, it provides only a fairly rough depiction of the course of the dance.

✔ For this reason, it's a good idea to videotape the performance as well.

✔ Is the theme itself divided into parts?

If you are unable to do this formal analysis yourself, you should seek help, for example from an experienced TEAM-dancer, a TEAM-dance judge, or a TEAM-dance trainer. You will quickly see what an enormous amount of time is saved by completing such a formal analysis. Often, when you have a new idea for a dance, you can tell at a glance that one piece of music or another is less suitable, or not at all suitable, because of formal reasons.

Experimenting

Despite the formal analysis, you will still need to experiment. At this stage, novices often have difficulty keeping the central musical theme and its interpretation at the forefront.

Modern interpretation offers you the freedom:

✔ to isolate a partial aspect and present it as a consistent whole;

✔ to juxtapose contrasting elements;

✔ to arrange individual elements in a sequence, which in turn may reflect the interpretation of a unifying theme.

Experimentation is thus not only the practical testing of various possibilities, but also the intellectual playing through of various statements.

Note: Don't make the mistake of trying to achieve a completely choreographed routine too soon. The experimental phase takes time, usually several months—especially when you are still inexperienced.

Every once in a while, of course, a choreographic work succeeds right away; it is simply so good that it cannot be improved upon. But this is rare, and it usually requires both creative talent and much experience. My advice: Give yourself time to experiment.

Choreography Program and Choreocell

Last of all comes the written choreography program. Each choreographed routine consists of standards, elements, movements or sequences, and figures. Unless the program is written down, the routine will look amateurish. The choreocell is a sketch of the performance as if seen from above, which helps you to visualize its progression. The individual musical segments are distinguished by different colors, and symbols represent special features.

Over time, a comprehensive and professional notation system has been developed for TEAM-

very easy to sketch out and review the intended use of space during the dance. Different segments of the music are indicated in different colors. The most important choreographic information is noted with letters or symbols.

✔ For better orientation, the eight directions are indicated.

✔ On the right margin, space is provided for notes about ideas for the dance, comments on specific figures, or reminders about future training plans.

TEAM-dance Notation

The notation comprises three parts:

✔ The top section shows the movements of the handler's upper body, head, and arms.

✔ The center section gives the sequence of steps and their direction.

✔ The bottom records what the dog is supposed to do.

Steps and pauses are indicated with traditional dance notation. Symbols, letters, and special notes round out the TEAM-dance notation to an almost complete medium for reproducing the performance on paper.

Four Steps to Performance

1. In the phase of choreographic sketching, you can start trying out and practicing individual sections with the dog—sometimes with music, sometimes not.

At the same time, you should learn your own part of the dance. When you know it fairly well, you can practice combining the dance with the verbal cues; do this without the dog at first.

Then take individual sections of the piece and rehearse them with the dog, starting slowly and without music. At the end of a successful passage, enjoy free play with music, as usual.

You, your dog, and music—the combination is an unforgettable experience.

dance, with specific templates that make the task much easier.

✔ The procedural section has spaces for essential information such as the choreographer, the date the choreography was begun, the handler and dog, the composer, the lyricist, the name, tempo, and length of the musical piece, and the TEAM-dance level.

✔ Below that is a space representing the dance ring, as if seen from above. It is drawn to scale on graph paper, with one square representing approximately one pace. This form makes it

Man and dog move together in the unison of variosynchronous pace.

Note: There is no point in trying to dance the entire piece when you are still having problems with individual sections.

2. Once your team has mastered the individual sections, you can start to link them together. Again, however, it is still too soon to try to perform the whole dance. As you join the sections, don't forget to be generous with praise when your dog performs well or even brilliantly. Those who begin to take the dog's achievements for granted and no longer reward them should not be surprised if their canine partner's motivation begins to dwindle.

The piece is not danced in its entirety until the final phase. Even then, you should intersperse periods of free play with the dog, some-times unpredictably. By keeping the element of surprise alive, you maintain a stronger inclination on the dog's part to stay concentrated without interruption.

Note: Be sure not to insist on peak performances at all times; rather, build up to an event or a task gradually. Occasional pauses, such as a break in training after an event, help restore creativity.

3. Have your performance reviewed. As you pull your piece together, you should occasion-

With a spring in its step, the dog follows its partner in time to the music.

ally ask experienced TEAM-dancers to watch a performance, or at least a videotape, and offer comments and suggestions. You will need the videotapes in any case as a memory aid (see TIP, page 54).

4. Practice with various distractions. Because dogs react differently to distractions, you should incorporate distractions such as stimulating sounds, sights, and odors as preparation for entering trials and tournaments. This might mean practicing in a different environment with different odors or unfamiliar people or dogs. When the dog's play instinct is strong, the risk of distraction is usually low.

For Advanced Dancers

Those who have completed TEAM-dance levels 1 and 2 may be intrigued by the thought of more advanced challenges. Any continuing study of dance—whether it be ballet, modern or jazz dance, folk dancing, or traditional ballroom dances—would be beneficial. It's important to keep in mind, however, that not everything you learn will carry over to TEAM-dance. Nevertheless, the further study of dance is always rewarding.

You can also learn from books and videos about dance, provided that you have the self discipline and patience to take what you see and try it out yourself in practice. The most productive way to pursue TEAM-dance at advanced levels, of course, is to take special courses in TEAM-dance and TEAM-dance choreography.

Developing TEAM Skills

Even more important than progressing as a dancer is developing TEAM skills. In performance levels 3 and 4, the handler and dog must master additional challenges:

✔ Dramatic and sudden movements by the handler must not distract the dog from its task, whether this is merely to hold still or to perform its own movement at the same time.

✔ Tasks at a distance become more frequent and more complex.

✔ The TEAM-dance cues must be communicated even more clearly.

✔ Nonverbal communication becomes more important.

Another problem arises out of the number and variety of the standards and their elements. Few dogs will be able to master all the elements of level 3 or 4. From time to time, it will be necessary to brush up on previous elements, as well as to refresh choreographed dances that might be performed again.

"ta-good"

A handler who is concentrating intently on the verbal cues and the dog's performance may often forget to praise the dog after a successful movement. A useful exercise is the verbal

The handler might also jump over the dog now and then.

"ta-good"! The handler learns to give praise at the right moment. However, this moment comes not at the end of a series of steps, but immediately after the first task has been completed, and that task is the very first step—the "ta". This is followed not by "tee," but by the accolade "good" (or similar praise).

Because we must not reward the dog only for the "ta" step, the cue "ta-good" is followed again by "ta," then "tee," and then "good" or free play. Soon the handler can begin to intersperse praise and play at irregular intervals, or, if the dog has a weak side, to polish those movements with greater emphasis and repetition.

Providing Variety

Steps that are repeated over and over become boring for the dog (and the handler) and lead to loss of concentration. It's a good idea to follow short sequences of steps with figures, and vice versa. You might take four steps forward, then "Stop" for both, another four steps forward, "Stop" for the dog and a figure for the handler,

then a solo figure for the dog and another four steps to a new position.

The Complete TEAM-dance

Variosynchronous pace is not a task for beginners, but rather a hallmark of advanced and highly advanced TEAM-dance. The handler and dog must feel their way gradually and mindfully toward this fascinating form of dancing in unison. It often takes years to progress from the earliest beginnings, when the dog keeps step with the handler once or twice in succession, to the most advanced form. But with every small progression toward this culminating form, dancing brings ever greater pleasure.

Variosynchronous pace is not required until TEAM-dance levels 3 and 4. The challenge is so

The challenge of dancing in formation—several teams dancing together.

complex that it cannot be described fully here. As in other aspects of TEAM-dance, ideally the dog should participate not just because success is followed by praise, but because the process itself is enjoyable. After the first footfall, there may be two, and then three and four footfalls in unison. The third footfall is especially important, because at that point the dog should learn to be familiar with uneven measures as well. After the expected number of footfalls in unison, there follows play or an immediate "Stop."

The numbers in bold face indicate color photos and illustrations.

Visible motivational objects are acceptable during practice sessions.

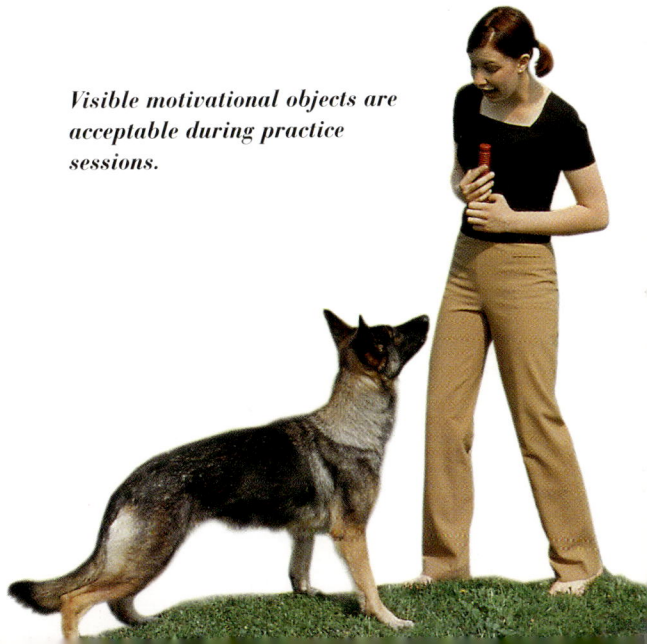

Helpful Addresses

The addresses below will direct you to a wealth of useful information; some are specific to canine freestyle while others are less-directly connected. However, if you and your dog are to successfully participate in canine freestyle, your dog must be physically able to perform the routines involved. Accordingly, all the following can benefit your canine dance partner.

American Dog Owners' Association
1654 Columbia Turnpike
Castleton, NY 12033

American Kennel Club
5580 Centerview Drive
Raleigh, NC 27606

American Temperament Testing Society
P.O. Box 397
Fenton, MO 63026

Canadian Kennel Club
89 Skyway Avenue
Suite 100
Etobicoke, Ontario
M9W 6R4

Canine Freestyle Federation Inc.
21900 Foxden Lane
Leesburg, VA 20175

Orthopedic Foundation for Animals (OFA)
2300 E. Nifong Blvd.
Columbia, MO 65201

United Kennel Club
100 East Kilgore Road
Kalamazoo, MI 49001-5593

World Canine Freestyle Organization
4547 Bedford Avenue
Brooklyn, NY 11235

Other Resources

For information about caring for your dog, consult your veterinarian, groomer or local humane society or dog club. The person from whom you acquired your dog or a well-qualified professional dog trainer can also be excellent sources of advice and information.

Worthwhile Websites and Web Pages

Like the worldwide web, canine freestyle is very new and most of the available information on this growing dog sport will be found in cyberspace. Happily, freestyle fans readily embrace the web, using it as a prime medium for the exchange of information. The list below features a number of sites and web pages directly related to canine freestyle and others that are for health issues and other training disciplines. Surf the Internet, and you will find many more interesting places to visit while you become more familiar with the pleasures of canine freestyle.

World Canine Freestyle Organization
http://www.woofs.org/wcfo

Canine Freestyle Federation
http://www.canine-freestyle.org/

IN-Style – Musical Freestyle
http://www.angelfire.com/ne/INStyle/

Animal CPR
http://members@aol.com/henryhbk/acpr.html

The Dog Obedience and Training Page
http://www.dogpatch.org/obed

National Animal Poison Control Center
http://www.napcc.aspca.org
[Tel: (800) 548-2423]

Versatile Dogs
http://www.versatiledogs.com

Recommended Reading

Books

D. Caroline Coile, Ph.D. *Encyclopedia of Dog Breeds.* Hauppauge, NY: Barron's Educational Series, Inc., 1998.

Sarah Whitehead. *The Complete Guide to the Dog.* Hauppauge, NY: Barron's Educational Series, Inc., 1999.

Ted Baer. *Communicating With Your Dog: A Humane Approach to Dog Training.* Hauppauge, NY: Barron's Educational Series, Inc., 1999.

Alison Hornsby. *All About Dog Training.* Hauppauge, NY: Barron's Educational Series, Inc., 1999.

Janet R. Lewis. *Smart Trainers – Brilliant Dogs.* Elkridge, MD: Canine Sports, No date

M. Christine Zink, DVM. *Peak Performance: Coaching the Canine Athlete.* Elkridge, MD: Canine Sports, 1997

Magazines

Dog World
500 North Dearborn
Suite 1100
Chicago, IL 60610

Dog Fancy
P.O. Box 6050
Mission Viejo, CA 92690

Northeast Canine Companion
P.O. Box 377
Sudbury, MA 01776

Front & Finish
P.O. Box 333
Galesburg, IL 61402-0333

About the Author

Ekard Lind is a widely respected college lecturer, a teacher, and one of the most interesting and sought-after authorities on the natural history of dogs in the world. His wealth of knowledge on the subject has provided him with the ideal background for understanding the most up-to-the- minute developments in the human-canine bond. Since 1990 he has developed two new dog-based sports disciplines. Dog owners who enjoy rhythmically moving to music will find in these formats a unique opportunity to engage in creative, dynamic interaction with their canine companions.

About the Photographers

The photographs in this book were taken by Marie-Therese, Maria and Ekard Lind.

Photographs on Cover and Full-Page Spreads:

Front cover: Variosynchronous pace—unmistakably TEAM-dance (large photo). Even without eye contact, both partners move in unison and in rhythm to the music (small photo). Back cover: TEAM-dance: An expression of harmony and affection. The bond between the two partners is evident. Page 1: Floor figures take the place of hurdles and other equipment. Pages 2–3: Following the model of ballroom dancing, the two TEAM partners maintain constant eye contact. Pages 4–5: Executing the figure "ring-around" with spirit and style. Pages 6–7: TEAM-dance in formation, with two pairs of partners in unison. Such precision takes years of practice. Pages 8–9: Dancing with dogs enhances the canine– human relationship. Pages 10–11: The fun is not limited to dancing—every dog enjoys a game of "fetch." Pages 12–13: Integral motivation, the Lind way: communication with gestures and verbal cues; moving together to the music; and finally, free play with the ball. Pages 14–15: The dog has just leaped over the girl; now she does a solo move, as her partner waits. Pages 16–17: The dog performs a "Spanish walk": left forepaw raised ("ta–ha"), right forepaw raised ("te–hee"). Page 64: The TEAM-partner dog completes a solo; the handler gives only verbal cues ("Start" "Under" "Stop" "Down").

English translation © Copyright 2001 by Barron's Educational Series, Inc.

Original title of the book in German is *TEAM-dance*

© Copyright 1999 by Gräfe und Unzer, Verlag, GmbH, Munich

English translation by Celia Bohannon

All rights reserved.
No part of this book may be reproduced in any form, by photostat, microfilm, xerography, or any other means, or incorporated into any information retrieval system, electronic or mechanical, without the written permission of the copyright owner.

All inquiries should be addressed to:
Barron's Educational Series, Inc.
250 Wireless Boulevard
Hauppauge, NY 11788
http://www.barronseduc.com

Library of Congress Catalog Card No. 00-107080

International Standard Book No. 0-7641-1737-8

Legal Disclosure

TEAM-dance represents a dog training system developed by Ekard Lind and trademarked as LIND-art®.

Printed in Hong Kong

9 8 7 6 5 4 3 2 1

1 Do I need musical talent to participate in TEAM-dance?

If you can move rhythmically to music, you have the basic talent you need. Extensive musical knowledge and skills are not necessary.

2 Can I start learning TEAM-dance with a dog that has already been trained?

Almost anything the dog can already do will transfer in some way to dance. Furthermore, a trained dog will enjoy learning something new.

3 Can my dog and I continue with more than one discipline at the same time?

Yes. Shortly before a competition, however, you should concentrate on one discipline. Use different cues for tasks that might be confused with each other.

4 Which breeds of dog are suitable for TEAM-dance?

In principle, all individuals and all breeds of dog are suitable for TEAM-dance.

5 Is TEAM-dance enough training for my dog?

No, because TEAM-dance does not cover all the areas in which dogs are motivated to learn.

Experts answer the 10 most common questions about TEAM-dance.

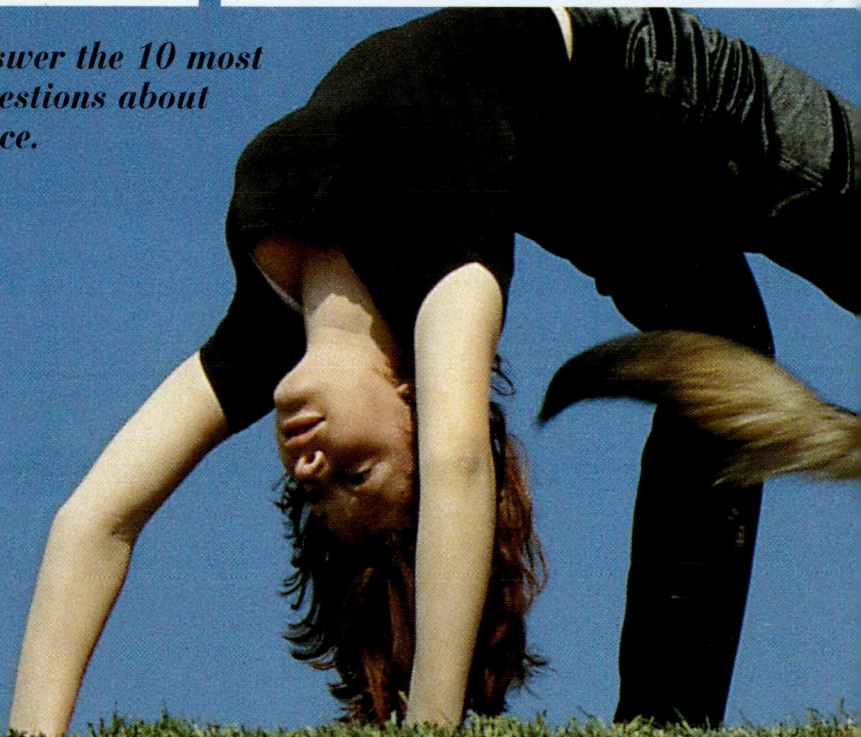